The Little Book of
Outside in A

Outdoor activities for the Foundation Stage

Written by Sally Featherstone
Illustrated by Sarah Featherstone

Little Books with ***BIG*** ideas®

The Little Book of Outside in All Weathers

ISBN 1-904187-57-9
978-1-904187-57-8

Series Editor, Sally Featherstone

First published in the UK, March 2003

Published in the United Kingdom by
Featherstone Education Ltd
44 - 46 High Street
Husbands Bosworth
Leicestershire
LE17 6LP

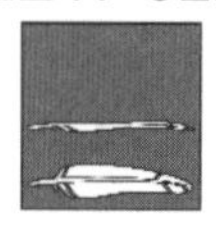

Introduction

The Little Book of Outside in all Weathers is an invitation to practitioners and children to enjoy the outside environment whatever the weather.

We have included things to do in the frost, snow, fog, wind, sun and rain. Many of the activities require a little preparation, or the collection of resources you already have. Involve the children in this preparation, and they will be more involved in the activities themselves. Encourage them to be inventive, adding and adapting resources and experimenting with new ideas.

The outdoor area (your garden) offers so much to children at all times of the year and in all weathers. Inclement weather should never be a reason for restricting children to the inside environment, and suitable clothing can easily be provided if you are inventive and persistent! Second hand boots, cheap parkas, sun hats, mittens can all be collected so children are never excluded from the exciting outdoors because they don't have the right clothing. Parents should understand that the outside environment is essential, a planned area where learning takes place, not just a place to let off steam and ride bikes!

Shelters and shade are important, and we give some guidance on how these can be made easily and cheaply. Craft and art activities can just as easily take place outside, and the more messy activities can often be better outside, where spills and drips can be washed away with a hose!

However, our major intention in this book is to encourage you to use the outside environment as an extension of your room, an exciting 'other place' for the Foundation curriculum.

Links with the Early Learning Goals

You will already know that a well planned and organised garden offers experience in all areas of learning.

Among other things, the activities in this book will enable children to:

* Explore and experiment (Knowledge and Understanding of the World);
* Make, construct, devise, join and fix things (Knowledge and Understanding of the World; physical);
* Observe nature and the weather (Knowledge and Understanding of the World);
* Run, jump, climb, ride etc. freely and vigorously (Physical);
* Explore colour, shape, form and space (Creative);
* Solve practical problems (Mathematical);
* Use tools and equipment (Physical, Technological);
* try new activities and work in groups (Personal and Social);
* Interact with others (Communication)
* Respond in a variety of ways (Creative)
* Find out about the place they live and the natural world (Knowledge and Understanding of the World);
* Make things (Technological)

The activities are all consistent with the Foundation Stage Guidance, and will also give you opportunities to observe learning in action.

Contents

Put the Wind to Work

Make some windmills

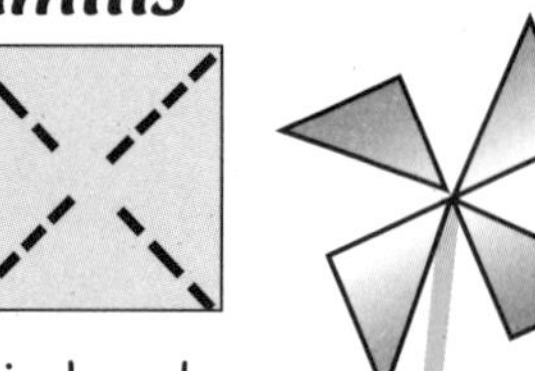

What you need:

* coloured paper
* scissors
* green garden sticks
* drawing pins or mapping pins with big heads

What you do:

1. Cut squares from the paper.
2. You could make patterns on the paper with crayons or chalk.
3. Fold the square from corner to corner to make guides, then cut from each corner to near the middle (you could draw pencil guide lines to help the children).
4. Bend each corner to the middle and pin to the stick. Make sure you leave the pin loose enough for the windmill to go round.
5. Go outside and test your toy!

Some other ideas for your windmills:

- Pin a row of windmills on the fence and watch them spin together.
- Fix windmills to the handlebars of bikes and scooters with elastic bands round the sticks.
- Make windmill hats on bands of card (fix them with split pins for safety) .
- Fix several windmills round a hoop and tie to the fence or a post.
- Make huge windmills from card or flexible plastic sheet, and put them in your garden.

and some other things:

- Make a weather centre in the garden. Put it where you can see it from inside. Pin a wind mill up, collect rain, hang a thermometer.
- Make wind wheels from paper plates or foil dishes. Make cuts all round the edges and fold them in. Pin the wheels to fences, trees, posts and watch them spin.
- Make cars or planes with Lego, Mobilo or other construction toys. Give them simple sails made from paper and small sticks, and let the wind whizz them along the path.
- Make some little boats from polystyrene and toothpicks. Give them sails and sail them along a piece of guttering filled with water.

Fly!

Make flying birds

These simple birds could even be made outside.

What you need:

* cardboard tubes (eg from kitchen roll) cut to about 10cm.
* scissors, white glue, felt pens
* feathers, string or wool
* paper and coloured sticky paper

What you do:

1. Turn the tubes into birds by covering with coloured paper.
2. Decorate them with feathers. You could look at some books for ideas or just let your imagination run riot with colours and feathers.
3. Add wings made from stiff paper, circles for eyes etc.
4. Make a tail from feathers.
5. Glue some wool or string to the head end of the tube.
6. Go outside and fly your birds in the garden.

Some other ideas for flying toys:

- Make some paper planes to fly outside.
- Make simple parachutes from squares cut from plastic carrier bags. Tie strings onto the corners and throw them into the wind with small world people or animals attached. See where they land.
- Make a simple kite from a carrier bag. Cut the end out of the bag. Turn it inside out and decorate with paint mixed with white glue, or with self adhesive stickers. Tie a string to the handles. Run in the wind to make it fly.

and some other things:

- Blow bubbles on a windy day, and see them fly away.
- In Autumn, fly sycamore 'helicopters' and other seeds with wings. Watch to see how the wings work to help the seed on its way.
- Do some 'flying things' spotting. Have a clip board or white board and record what you see - birds, planes, butterflies, helicopters, balloons etc.
- Sit and watch the clouds racing across the sky. Look for shapes and pictures in the clouds. Watch how they change as they blow around.
- Read 'The Blue Balloon'.

Make a Sound

Make a wind chime

What you need:

* metal objects (spoons, forks, foil trays, coins, buckles, metal buttons, etc.)
* scissors, string
* a coat hanger or small hoop
* a large feather, a cork or a big bead

What you do:

1. Hang the metal things from the hanger or hoop with string.
2. Check they are near enough to strike, but far enough away not to get their strings tangled.
3. Hang one longer string in the middle with a feather, cork or bead on the end (to catch the wind).
4. Hang your wind chime in a tree, on a bush, a climbing frame or from a hook in the wall. Try different places for the best effect.

Some other ideas for sound in your garden:

- Hang old saucepan lids and metal kitchen tools in bushes or in the gaps between the fence. Use a wooden spoon to make music.
- Hang old CDs on strings for a gentle sound.
- Buy bells of different sizes and hang these singly or in groups.
- Look for wind chimes at a garden centre or 'pound shop'. Autumn and January sales are good times!
- Make a chime with lengths of bamboo or metal tubes hung on strings of different lengths attached to a coat hanger.

and some other things:

- Let the wind make sounds in tubes and bottles.
- Take some simple musical instruments outside and have a marching band round the garden to let off steam! Sing 'We Can Play on a windy day, and this is the way we do it. Bang, bang, bang on a windy day and this is the music to it.'
- Read 'The Happy Hedgehog Band.'
- Find a collection of stories about windy days, such as 'When the Wind Blew', 'Mrs Mopple's Washing Line'.
- Put up a pop up tent or other wind break and talk about how to shelter from the wind.

Flap and Wave

Make bunting and flags

What you need:

* plastic carrier bags (different colours are nice if you can find them)
* scissors, permanent markers
* string
* stapler

What you do:

1. Help the children to cut shapes from the carrier bags (squares, rectangle, strips, triangles).
2. You could fringe the edges of some of the shapes, or draw patterns with the markers.
3. Cut a long piece of string and staple the shapes firmly to the string.
4. Go outside and hang your flags up in the wind.

Some other ideas:

- Add some small foil dishes or old CDs to the bunting.
- Make bunting from triangles made from scraps of fabric.
- Make long strips of plastic or fabric and write the children's names on them.
- Make a set of flags to hang between the trees or fence.
- Make flags for the climbing frame. Tie them on sticks and attach with elastic or string. Make your climbing frame into a castle or pirate ship.

and some other things:

- Tie strips of fabric to the handlebars of trikes and scooters.
- Make a banner to hang outside the door to celebrate a special day, or to tell parents about what you have done today.
- Make a 'wind sock' from a small carrier bag to add to your weather station (see p4).
- Look at flag books and design some flags of your own.
- Make or buy some national flags and add these to your outside role play collection.
- Make little flags on cocktail sticks to go on top of sand or mud pies, or make signs, directions and notices.

Wet and Dry

Make a car wash on a windy day

What you need:

* wheeled toys
* buckets, sponges, rollers, brushes, cloths, old towels, hose
* bubble bath, aprons or overalls, wellies
* playground chalk, plastic money, clip board, pen, 'tickets'

What you do:

1. Help the children to organise the car wash. Use chalk to make a waiting line. Make some tickets.
2. Mix the bubble bath with some warm water.
3. Help them decide who are going to be the washers. Agree ways of taking turns, playing etc.
4. Use the bubbly water and the tools to wash the toys. Leave them in the wind to dry.
5. Make sure you build in clearing up time!

Some other ideas for drying things in your garden:

- Paint with water and watch the wind dry it.
- Have a washing day, where you wash equipment and use the wind to dry it.
- Wash the dolls' clothes and put up a washing line to dry them on.
- Even if you have a washing machine in your setting, use windy days to dry things outside.
- Make some puddles on purpose. Draw round them with chalk and watch them dry up in the wind. You could draw a new circle round the puddle every hour, and measure the difference as the puddle dries.

and some other things:

- Take a water tray outside for washing all sorts of things from inside.
- Dip different sorts of fabrics in water, hang them on a washing line and see how long they take to dry.
- Go for a walk in the park or somewhere else in the neighbourhood and feel the wind in your hair.
- Put out a paddling pool, fill it with water and watch the wind make waves. Add some sailing boats.
- Have a doll's hairdresser's outside and wash the dolls hair. Let the wind dry it.

What Can You See & Hear?

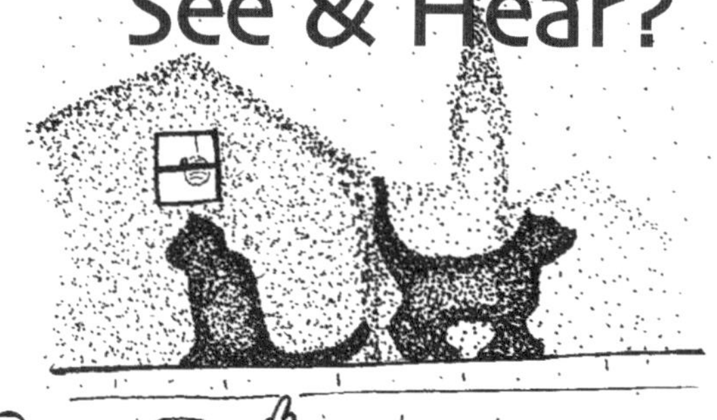

Looking for shapes in the fog

What you need:

* clip board and pen (or several smaller ones for older children)
* a small group of children
* a picture clue sheet of all the things you might see.
* a camera (not essential)

What you do:

1. Talk with the children about what you might see or hear in the fog.
2. Go for a walk and record what you see and hear (either by ticking, drawing or writing a list).
3. Talk about how different things look and sound in the fog.
4. Look at colours and shapes.
5. Use words like misty, dim, muffled, grey, moist, faraway, echo, fuzzy, etc.

Some other ideas for a foggy day:

- Have some torches out. Fix some to the bikes for fog lights.
- Make some fog horns with cardboard tubes and cones (hosiery cones make fantastic foghorns). Decorate them with thick felt pens or painted patterns, or stick ribbons or streamers.
- Get some bike hooters (from a bike shop) and keep them for foggy days. Fix them to handlebars or give them to children to hoot!
- Collect some old glasses frames, remove the lenses and put tracing paper over to make 'fog glasses'.

Art in the Fog

Make foggy day pictures on a window

What you need:

* black paper
* white, pale blue, grey and black tissue
* paste or very dilute white glue, spreaders

What you do:

1. Go outside and have a good look at the fog and how it changes the way things look. Look at the edges of buildings, the outlines of objects, the fuzzy nature of what you can see.
2. Now go back into the room and look at the materials you could use for a picture on the window.
3. Help the children to tear the tissue and paste it on the window in a pattern or picture.
4. Don't be tempted to cut shapes out, the torn edges will make the picture or pattern look suitable fuzzy, and the children will find it easier to do!

Some other ideas for foggy days:

- Make foggy day pictures with a limited range of paint (grey, white, black, pale blue) on grey paper.
- Make pictures on tracing paper with very thin paint in grey and black. When the picture is done, rub the back of the tracing paper with a little cooking oil on a cotton wool ball to make it transparent. Display on a window or against a light.
- Sponge print by dabbing on a window or mirror in grey and white paint. Then stick black cutouts of cats and dogs on top of the paint. Try putting the cats on top of a wall.

❄ Dig, Shape and Mould

Make some snow moulds

What you need:

- * small tubs, plastic cups, pots, sand moulds, small jelly moulds, bun tins, etc.
- * a table, empty water tray or builder's tray outside
- * spoons, scoops, sand toys, spatulas, blunt knives etc
- * buckets, spades, shovels
- * mittens or gloves (if you put plastic or rubber gloves underneath mittens, hands stay warm for longer)

What you do:

1. Scoop some snow into the buckets and transfer to the tray.
2. Use the snow to make cakes, pies, moulds and castles.
3. Use spoons and other tools to make textures and to cut the shapes in the snow. decorate with leaves, twigs and stones.
4. Make shops, do cooking, have parties or just play!

Some other ideas for using snow:

- Use rakes or sticks to draw or make patterns in the snow.
- Use blunt knives to cut bricks for a miniature igloo.

- Make sculptures of people, faces, animals or vehicles in snow.
- Put snow in an empty sand tray and add small world people, vehicles or zoo animals.

- Try making a snow car or bus that you can really ride in!
- Make hollows in the snow, pack it tight, fill with very cold water and leave over night to freeze.

and some other things:

- Press leaves, twigs and stones into snow to make patterns.
- Take a tape player outside and play 'The Snowman' music.

- Bring the camera and take photos of the fun.
- Read a snowy story outside - eg 'The Snowy Day',

- Put up a pop up tent or make a shelter with a sheet. Get inside and see how it feels. Play Arctic explorers with a sleeping bag and rucksack.

- Everyone could help to make a huge snow castle (a sandcastle with snow - decorate with things you find outside).

Colour It!

Colour the snow!

What you need:

- * small hand operated spray bottles
- * empty plastic bottles with lids
- * water with food colouring added or very runny paint
- * string

What you do:

1. Make holes in the tops of bottles, and tie a string round some of them.
2. Fill the bottles and sprays with pint or coloured water.
3. Go outside. Spray or drizzle colour on the snow.
4. Try making patterns and pictures.
5. Watch how the colours mix and melt into the snow.

NOTE: *put an old towel or plenty of newspaper by the door for painty, drippy feet as they come in!*

Some other ideas for snow painting:

- Use brushes to paint in the snow.
- Tear some strips and shapes of tissue and crepe paper. Lay these on the snow and leave for a few minutes. Remove the paper and the colour should be left behind.
- Use thick paint to paint the ice on shallow puddles or trays of water left out over night.
- Freeze some ice cubes or shapes. You could put small objects (beads, sequins, berries etc) in them. When they are frozen, put them in a water tray outside on a cold day and watch what happens as the children play with them.

and some other things:

- Drip thick paint onto a frozen puddle and see what happens as it freezes.
- Sing 'This is the way we colour the snow' to the tune of 'Here We Go Round the Mulberry Bush'.
- Fill some ice cube trays with water and add a few drops of food colouring. Freeze the cubes and see what happens to the colouring.
- Buy a bag of ice from a supermarket for a different sort of water tray experience. You could also provide spray bottles of dilute food colouring or paint to spray the cubes. Do this on a cold day so the ice lasts longer.

Make Your Mark

Go on a Tracking Walk

What you need:

* a clip board or note book and pen
* binoculars or a digital camera (optional)
* a guide to birds and animals (and their tracks if possible)
* bird food or breadcrumbs

What you do:

1. Before you leave, talk with the children about what you are looking for and where they might find tracks and trails of animals and birds. Remind them that they will need to look and walk very carefully so they don't frighten the creatures or obliterate their tracks!
2. Visit part of your grounds, a park, field or path where there are likely to be animal or bird prints. You could scatter some bird food (even before you go), to attract wildlife. Record what you find.

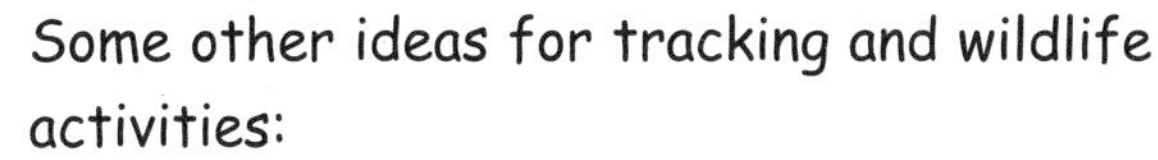

Some other ideas for tracking and wildlife activities:

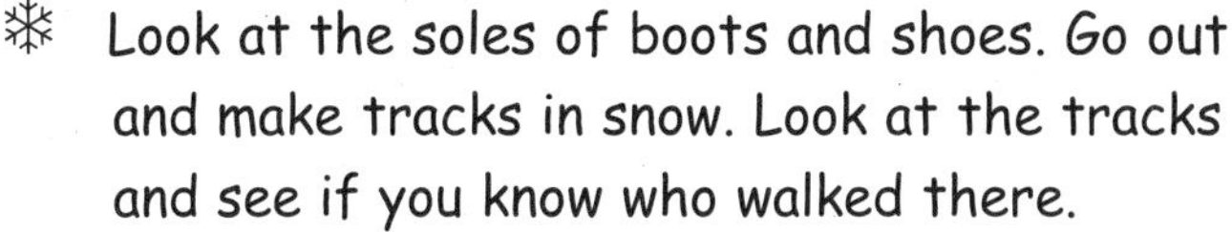

- Look at the soles of boots and shoes. Go out and make tracks in snow. Look at the tracks and see if you know who walked there.

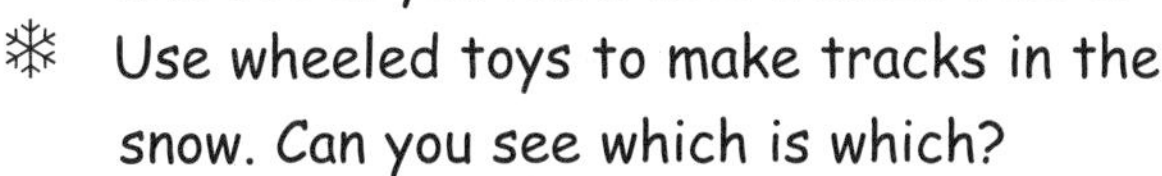

- Use wheeled toys to make tracks in the snow. Can you see which is which?

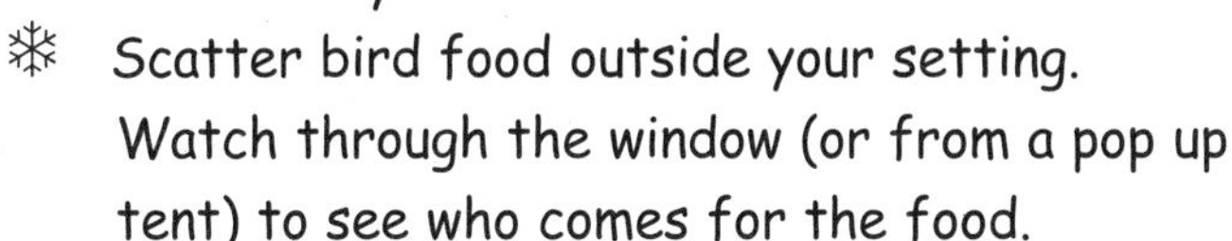

- Scatter bird food outside your setting. Watch through the window (or from a pop up tent) to see who comes for the food.

- Take small world figures and animals out in the snow to make their own tracks. Make a snow scene in a builders' tray, with diggers, dumper trucks and people.

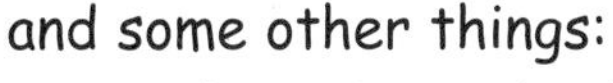

and some other things:

- Make or buy a bird table to stand on the path or grass, or to hang in a tree. You can make a hanging bird table from a small wooden vegetable box. Tie thin ropes to the corners and knot these together to hang from a tree, bush or hook in the wall.

- Make a bird feeder from an empty plastic drinks bottle. Push some sticks through the bottle for the birds to perch on. Cut some small holes near the perches to peck through.

- Make some bird cake by mixing wild bird food with melted fat. Pour into a bowl and leave to set before tipping out on the bird table for the birds to eat.

Move It!

Find a place to sledge and slide

What you need:

* a safe place - flat or with a gentle slope
* plastic sledges or trays or thick plastic sacks
* strong string or thin rope
* a camera

What you do:

1. Talk to the children about good, safe places to slide and sledge. These might include the local park, a field, or even some kind neighbour's garden.
2. Make sure everyone is warmly dressed and well padded for spills! Have plenty of adults with you.
3. New snow is good for sledging - go out as soon as it falls if you can.

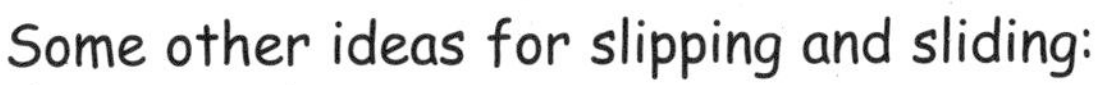

Some other ideas for slipping and sliding:

- Leave a tray of water out overnight to freeze. Make it into a miniature ice skating rink with small world people.
- Fill a tray with snow and make a skiing scene with people and vehicles. Make some sleighs from very small boxes, and make an ice rink with a mirror.
- Use counters or draughts to make an outdoor sliding game in a tray of ice.
- Make sledges from Lego or other construction toys to slide on frozen puddles or trays of ice.
- Turn large brick play into a sledge and play at expeditions to the Frozen North.

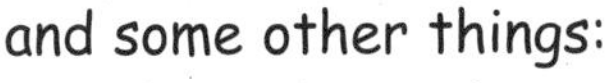

and some other things:

- Paint snowy pictures outside.
- Tie long streamers of crepe paper round children's ankles and let them stream through the snow - the colour will follow them as the paper gets damp!
- Fill a plastic tray with water and freeze it. Now melt some chocolate, and while it is still liquid, carefully pour it onto the ice. The chocolate will quickly set hard, so you can make letters and shapes to eat immediately. Talk about what happens to the chocolate as it gets very cold.
- Give the children some plastic beach spades to dig and move the snow.

Close Up

Get up close to snow

What you need:

* magnifying glasses (one each if possible)
* black paper or fabric
* falling snow
* camera
* small groups of children

What you do:

1. Make sure children know how to use a magnifying glass and what it can do.
2. Go outside and let the snow fall on your clothes and faces. Some children will stick out their tongues to taste it too!
3. Help the children to look at the snow falling on their sleeves. Put some black paper on a flat surface to catch some snowflakes. Look at the flakes through the magnifiers. Talk about what you see.

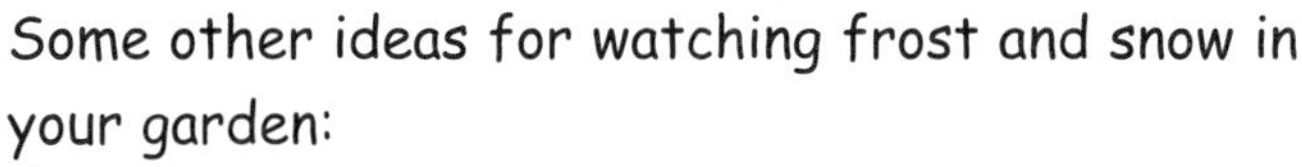

Some other ideas for watching frost and snow in your garden:

- Look at frost on a window.
- Use a magnifying glass to look at frost or snow on a spider's web.
- Watch drops form on icicles or the ends of branches as the ice and snow melt.
- Look up as snow falls and talk about what you see.
- Watch snow and ice melt. Take 'time lapse' photos as snow and ice disappear.
- Look at things covered with snow and guess what they are. Watch the snow melt and uncover the object bit by bit.

and some other things:

- Make frost pictures with very salty water. Paint with the solution then dry the picture to reveal the sparkly salt.
- Put a big bag of salt in a tray. Paint a design on a piece of black card with white glue. Put the card in the tray and completely cover with the salt. Lift the picture out and tip off excess salt. Dry in a warm place. The salt will dry sparkly.
- Make Puffy Paint by mixing 4 cups flour, 4 cups water and 4 cups salt. Mix well. Use this paint to make snowy day pictures. The paint puffs up and looks like snow. Don't forget you can paint outside even in the winter.

Freeze It! Melt It!

Make some ice hangings

What you need:

* shallow lids from yogurt and margarine tubs
* scissors, wool or thin string
* greenery - holly, evergreeen leaves, berries, sticks and twigs from the garden (or a practitioner's garden!).
* water

What you do:

1. Snip leaves etc and make a pattern in the lid.
2. Fill the lid with water, and put a piece of wool or string in to make a hanger (ends in water, loop hanging out)
3. Put in the freezer or leave outside overnight to freeze.
4. Take out of the mould and hang in trees and bushes.
5. Make some with bird food for the birds to peck at. Hang them from your bird table.

These hangings look lovely with a light behind them!

Some other ideas for freezing in your garden:

- Make an ice bowl for your bird table. It will slowly melt and release the bird food! You need two bowls that fit inside each other. In the bigger one, put some wild bird food. Add some water and put the smaller bowl inside. Weight this down so the water fills the space between the bowls without overflowing.
  Freeze the whole lot - and then take both bowls off, leaving a bowl of ice!
  Put the bowl on your bird table, fill it with more bird food and watch what happens!
- *Don't forget to put out water every day.*

and some other things:

- Try freezing small things in puddles - glitter, small beads, leaves and grasses, seeds.
- Put some plastic bottles outside. Part fill them with coloured water. Mark the water level with a permanent marker and leave out on a frosty night. Look in the morning and see what has happened.
- After a hard frost, look for icicles hanging from roofs and guttering. Talk about how they are formed.
- Hang some wet dolls' clothes outside on a washing line. Leave over a frosty night (or in the freezer) and discuss what has happened in the morning.

Jump, Splash, Sweep

Find a puddle and have some fun!

What you need:

* wellington boots
* brooms - child sized
* playground chalk
* small sponge balls or sponges

What you do:

1. Make sure everyone has boots on - it's impossible to stay out of a puddle when you are having fun!
2. Firstly, just let the children wade and walk in the puddle, exploring how it feels.
3. Now draw a line on the ground a little distance from the puddle and play throwing the sponge balls into the puddle. fetching the balls is even more fun than throwing them!
4. Next, offer the children the brooms and brushes to sweep the water so the puddle disappears.

Some other ideas for using a puddle:

- Try puddle jumping over small puddles.
- Collect some plastic or wooden boats and sail them on the puddle.
- Use outdoor bricks and large construction to make bridges and stepping stones over the puddles.
- Use buckets and cups to collect all the water and move it somewhere else - to a drain, a flower bed, a plant tub, a water butt.
- Use the water to paint with.
- Ride bikes and scooters through the puddle to make tracks on the path or yard. Make wellie tracks as well.

and some other things:

- Use a hose to fill a hollow or puddle place, giving the children sweeping practice.
- Add bubble bath to a puddle and whisk up a foam with whisks and beaters.
- Read a rainy story outside. How about 'Alfie's Boots'?
- March around the puddles singing rainy songs (with or without instruments). Weather songs are at the end of the book.
- Make a rain gauge for your Weather Station. Cut an empty plastic drinks or washing up liquid bottle here. Reverse the top bit into the bottom to form a collecting funnel.

Add It!

Add some things to puddles and rain

What you need:

* two or three of the following additives - sand, bubbles, washing up liquid, glitter, food colouring, tissues, dry pasta, dry spaghetti, dried peas, paint, gravel, flour
* wet path, small puddle or container of rain
* magnifying glasses, camera

What you do:

1. Work with a small group to add things to your rain puddle.
2. Add one thing at a time and give the children time to watch what happens.
3. Take photos or record what happens by tape recording or writing what the children say.
4. Talk about the things that change when they get wet and the ones that don't; things that float and things that sink.

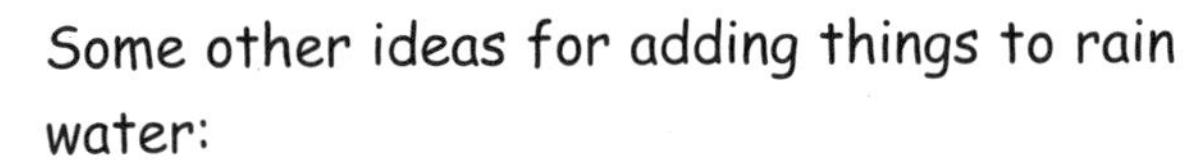

Some other ideas for adding things to rain water:

- Scoop some rain water into a few margarine pots and add some washing up liquid. Cut a nick near the top of some straws (to stop them sucking by mistake!). Blow bubbles in the water and then pour the bubbly water on the ground, on paper, on sand, on pavings. Watch what happens.
- Collect rain or find a puddle and put in some blue or green colouring. Sail boats on the sea.
- Add some wallpaper paste to a puddle and see what happens as you stir it. Adding a few drops of colouring makes it even more fun.

and some other things:

- Put an unbreakable mirror on the ground and watch the raindrops fall on it.
- Use some wet spaghetti to make pictures - you don't need to cook it, just soak it in a pool of water. It will stick to the paper (or a a mirror or window) with its own starch!
- Do finger painting on a wet table or sheet of plastic. Remember to wear an apron!
- Find a puddle or collect some rainwater. Mix some cooking oil and ink (or get some marbling ink) and marble some sheets of paper.
- Soak some crumbled chalk in rain water and use it to paint on the path. Wash it off with a hose, or wait for more rain.

Make it Move!

Make a waterway

What you need:

* guttering and drainpipes, waterproof tape, scissors
* funnels and tubing, bowls and possibly a paddling pool
* watering cans, buckets, jugs and other containers
* wellies and waterproof clothing, camera

What you do:

This activity is best done on a rainy day - they are going to get wet anyway! You could do it on a hot day too!

1. Talk with the children about all the things they can use.
2. Suggest that they might like to make a waterway construction to collet the rain.
3. Help them to fix the construction, but try not to interfere. Experimenting is part of the fun.
4. Encourage the children to test and adapt their construction, and bring some extra water out if there is not enough rain.

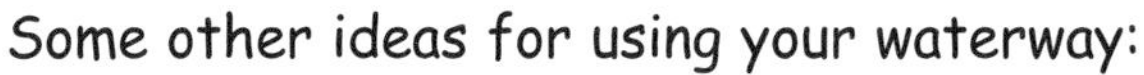

Some other ideas for using your waterway:

- Offer children some boats to sail along the waterway.
- Make boats in the technology area to sail outside.
- Make bridges and tunnels, waterfalls, locks and docks.
- Add some cranes and see if your boats can carry tiny cargo.
- Offer waterwheels and talk about other ways of moving water.
- Try to visit a canal, river or dock to see real waterways at work, or watch a video such as Rosie and Jim.

and some other things:

- Put water wheels in the water tray.
- Tell some stories about rivers and water: 'Rosie and Jim', 'Little Quack', 'The Little Boat', 'Noah's Ark', "Master salt the Sailor'.
- Make big bricks or your climbing frame into a role play boat, and have some adventures.
- Sing songs about water - 'Row Your Boat', 'A Sailor Went to Sea, Sea, Sea', 'Bobby Shaftoe', 'The Big Ship Sails'.
- Go and find some drainpipes on your setting and talk about what they are for, and how they work. Look at drains, watch water running along the pavement and into the gutter.

Float and Sink

Try floating and sinking in the rain

What you need:

* a bowl or bath on a table, a water trolley or deepish puddle
* collected rain or tap water
* a basket of items to experiment with. Some ideas - corks, plastic bottles with tops, stones and pebbles, leaves, wooden and plastic bricks, metal and plastic spoons, plastic boxes
* two containers to sort the objects into

What you do:

1. Give the children plenty of time to explore the objects in the water, before discussing floating and sinking.
2. Spend plenty of time watching and discussing the activity.
3. When the children are ready, help them to sort the objects into floaters and sinkers.

NB. A board across the water tray is useful for resting things on.

Some other ideas for water experiments:

- Put some boats in the water tray or puddle, see if they float or sink, and if you can load them with little stones or sticks.
- Test other things from the classroom or nursery. Find things in the garden to try.
- Offer some clip boards or white boards for recording their findings.
- Try other things, polystyrene wiggles, tooth picks, bits of cork tile, plastic, card. Talk about things that float to start with, then get waterlogged and begin to sink. Look at things that float just below the surface when waterlogged.

and some other things:

- Talk about lifeboats and life belts. Make some life belts for play people and rescue them from the water.
- Go to the park and look at the ducks. How do they stay afloat?
- Watch boats on a river or on a video or TV.
- Find a safe bridge and play the game from Winnie The Pooh called 'Pooh Sticks'. Find a stick each and drop it over into the water on one side of the bridge, Run to the other side of the bridge and see whose stick wins the race under the bridge.

  Read the story or watch the video when you get back.

Drips and Drops

Make drippy pictures in the rain

What you need:

* paper
* food colouring or water based inks (several colours)
* plastic droppers or soft paint brushes
* boards and masking tape
* water (for emergency use if it isn't raining hard enough!)

What you do:

1. Tape paper on the boards.
2. Take the boards outside and let them get wet.
3. Put some food colouring into small containers.
4. Prop the boards up so they are sloping (put a brick under one end). Spray with water if necessary so the paper is wet).
5. Dip the droppers in the colouring and drip onto the boards so the colour runs down the paper. Use several colours so they make a rainbow. Place flat to dry.

Some other ideas for drips and drops:

- Have raindrop races down the windows.
- Use all sorts of containers to make drips and drops - sieves, colanders, bottles with holes in them, water bottles, sponges.
- Put big sheets of paper, plastic or card on the ground and sprinkle them with powder paint. Let the rain drip on them or drip water on from droppers.
- Put simple containers under gutters, under the corner of buildings, anywhere the rain drips off. Watch the drips fall into the containers and the patterns they make on the surface of the water.

and some other things:

- Make some dripping music with bells and metal objects. Hang them on strings outside for even more fun.
- Watch the 'Drip, Drop, Drip Little April Shower' rain sequence from the 'Bambi' film.
- Use guttering and pipes to make dripping waterways - use real rain if possible.
- Put plain sheets of grey or coloured paper on the path and watch the raindrops fall in a pattern.
- Put an unbreakable mirror on the ground and watch the rain falling on its surface.
- Make a dripping water clock from a plastic bottle with a very small hole in it.

Sponge, Squeejee, Scrape

Paint with squeejees and scrapers

What you need:

* aprons!
* finger paint, thick card to make your own squeejees
* squeejees and scrapers (the sort used on car windscreens)
* a smooth flat surface such as a table top
* paper to take prints (optional)

What you do:

1. Pour some paint on the table top.
2. Use the scrapers and squeejees to make patterns in the paint.
3. Add finger marks and swirls, marks with brushes, combs and other kitchen objects.
4. Take a print of the pattern if you like, by putting some paper over the pattern and smoothing it <u>gently</u> before removing it.
5. This method is good for backings for a watery display.

Some other ideas for using sponges and squeejees:

- Squeejee the classroom windows with a window cleaner's squeejee and a bucket of water.
- Drop sponges soaked in water or runny paint on big sheets of paper.
- Make a maths game to play with sponges. Get a few buckets and paint numbers or shapes on them. Throw wet or dry sponges into the buckets from a starting line, and score accordingly.
- Clean the bikes and other toys with sponges and buckets of warm soapy water. Dry and polish them.

and some other things:

- Fix sponges to your wellies with big elastic bands. Walk in a shallow tray of paint or water, then walk or jump across a piece of paper or board.
- Do sponge printing with water on walls and paths.
- Use sponges to mop up water from pools, trays and puddles. Collect the water in a bucket.
- Have a collection of different sorts of sponges in a water tray. Use them for squeezing and squishing - it's great for strengthening finger and hand muscles.

Squirt, Spray, Wash, Paint

Spray away!

What you need:

* several small plastic spray bottles
* very liquid paint or water with food colouring
* very large sheets of paper (rolls of wallpaper will do)
* somewhere to fix the paper so it is vertical

What you do:

1. Pin or fix the big sheets of paper to a wall, fence, shed or door. This is a collaborative activity!
2. Fill the spray bottles with several colours of paint. make sure it is very liquid.
3. Spray away! The resulting pattern will run down the paper and the colours will merge to make a wonderful rainbow design.
4. Try spraying the paper with water first.

Some other ideas for using sprays and squirters:

- Cover up well and use the sprays to spray each other (willing participants only!).
- Spray bikes and other toys with temporary colourings. Wash off with a hose.
- Chalk some shapes on the ground or wall and spray fill them with paint or water.
- Spray water or paint on pieces of fabric or plastic, pegged on a washing line.
- Spray water on windows and use a squeejee to scrape it off.
- Use sprays to water plants and bushes, to wash paths and paving stones, to bring the colour back to dusty leaves.

and some other things:

- You could have a garden spray working on a rainy day. Make sure everyone is water-proofed!
- Find some net and other fabrics with holes in (fruit bags, garden net, curtain net or lace). Put these on paper and spray over them. Remove the fabrics to reveal the patterns.
- Try the same thing with objects. Put flattish objects, (eg shapes, animals, pencils, bricks, crayons) on paper, spray over them and remove to reveal their silhouettes. Try this with white paint on black paper.

Collect It!

Collect the rain while you are outside

What you need:

* a range of plastic or metal containers (some big, some small, some with narrow necks, some with wide, bowls, jugs, jars, bottles, tins etc)
* sticks or rulers to measure the water (optional)
* chalk board or clip board, paper, markers, playground chalk

What you do:

1. Talk with the children about how you could collect the rain and which containers would be best.
2. Find some good places to leave the containers and agree which ones go where. You could draw round them with chalk to make sure they stay put!
3. Visit the containers and talk about the best collecting places, the best containers, why some look fuller than others etc. Help them record what they find out.

Some other ideas for collecting rain:

- Buy a water butt and set it up in your garden. Try putting it under a down pipe. Use the rain water to water your plants.
- If it rains hard, try making a water course with different levels and different sorts of pipes and tubes. Try changing the course of the water by moving the equipment.
- Collect some rain water in a big container, or a hollow in the ground. See whether any wildlife comes for a drink. You may find snails, slugs, or even something bigger has been. If it is muddy nearby, look for foot-prints of birds and animals.

and some other things:

- Look for places where puddles collect and talk about why this happens.
- Make rain collecting systems and objects for your weather station.
- Talk about funnels and other ways of diverting rain into collecting places. Experiment with these. Offer the children a wide range of construction items to make collecting systems.
- Dig some small holes or hollows in the earth and collect water from rain to make pools or puddles.
- Leave some containers outside overnight and see what you have collected by morning.

Shelter

Make shelters from the rain

What you need:

* a large sheet of plastic, preferably transparent (a cheap shower curtain is good value)
* bricks or large stones
* a rope or pole between two fixing points, or two supports such as painting easels, trolleys or climbing apparatus
* a blanket, some old carpet or carpet samples

What you do:

1. Fix the pole or rope firmly in position with string or roof-rack elastics
2. Drape the plastic over the rope and hold the edges down with bricks (or peg it into the grass).
3. Spread the carpet or blanket inside and enjoy the hideout!
4. Add a basket with picnic things, or a rucksack with bird watching kit.

Some other ideas for making rainy day shelters:

- Put up a gazebo for big groups, and have a table and chairs underneath.
- Tie some garden canes together at the top. Wrap with plastic or a sheet to make a tepee.
- Put a pop up tent just outside the door and join it to the inside by a play tunnel, so children can go out without even getting wet!
- Put a big sheet of plastic over a climbing frame or other large structure.
- Make a shelter by screwing a batten on the wall. Then hook plastic or fabric to the batten and hold the edge of the fabric down with bricks.

and some other things:

- Put big pieces of foil on umbrellas and hear the raindrops falling on the top.
- Tie a big golf umbrella to a post or the climbing frame to provide shelter.
- Frame tents are cheap and don't need pegging down.
- Fill some buckets with ready mixed concrete, push a broom handle in each, and leave to dry. Use these stands for umbrellas, or for tying fabric or plastic sheets to.
- Even a couple of tables covered with a sheet will make an exciting place to play in the rain. Children will love the new place to imagine and explore in role with just a few props.

Pool and Cool

Make a pool for a hot day

What you need:

* a big sheet of plastic (pool liner is best, but any tough plastic will do)
* big stones, bricks or soil, spades and trowels
* lots of newspaper

What you do:

1. Find a place where there is a dip in the ground (eg where rain collects). A place on the grass is ideal - or you could dig a shallow dip in the earth.
2. Put a thick layer of newspaper down in the area to stop the plastic tearing.
3. Cover the paper with plastic and weight the edges down with stones or bricks. If you are making the pond on the flat, use bricks both under and over the edge of the plastic.
4. Fill with water ad enjoy!

Some other ideas for cooling down on really hot days:

- Pump up a paddling pool and use it for paddling, or for floating boats.
- Or use the pool empty for pool painting. Cover the bottom of the empty paddling pool with paper, dip soft balls, toy cars, marbles etc in paint and roll around to make painty patterns.
- Fill a water tray or paddling pool with ice cubes (buy them in bulk from a freezer centre).
- Get some child sized watering cans and use them to water gardens, paths, walls or plants.
- Put a bubble fountain on a table or the ground and let the children explore the spray with their hands and faces.

and some other things:

- Make some simple water bombs from disposable rubber gloves. Fill with water, tie the ends and throw up in the air or at a wall. If you cover the wall with paper or a sheet, you can fill the bombs (or sponges) with paint and make a splatted mural.
- Fill small spray bottles with playing water so children can cool their own faces, hands, arms and legs.
- Put some smooth, polished pebbles in small bowls of water for a soothing activity.
- Remember to provide cups or bottles of water for drinking on hot days, and to encourage children to drink frequently.

Shelter and Shade

Make some home made shade

What you need:

* four broom handles or strong canes
* string, clothes pegs or elastic bands
* thin material (gauze, sari fabric, net curtain)
* a blanket or piece of carpet

What you do:

1. Net, voile or gauze are quite heavy enough to make shade, and they are easier for children to manage when they make their own shelters.
2. Fix the broom handles firmly in the ground, or set them in concrete (see page 51).
3. Tie, peg or band the fabric to the four posts to make a sort of flat lid.
4. Spread a blanket under your gazebo and use it for reading, picnics, story time or small world play.

Some other ideas for making shade:

- Use a beach wind break (or fabric walls attached to posts or canes). This will provide a surprising amount of shade.
- Cover climbing equipment with big sheets, netting or shower curtains.
- Find a shady spot under a tree, near a wall or by a fence. Put a sheet of plastic or an old carpet down and use for floor play such as bricks, cars, small world.
- Fix parasols and umbrellas to posts and fences to provide pools of shade for individuals and small groups.
- Make miniature tents for small world and dolls.

and some other things:

- Buy some rush matting or garden wind break (this comes in a many types of natural materials). Attach to fences to make natural looking, more permanent shade.
- Grow climbers up fences and over walls to make additional shade. Make arbours, tunnels and corners of leafy shade.
- Provide hats, visors and individual child size umbrellas on sunny days. Encourage children to be inventive about creating shade.
- Use your shed or play storage area to provide shade for bigger groups of children, or for a large role play area. (If it is in a muddle, this is a good reason to clear it out!)

What Can The Sun Do?

Magic pictures - by sun power!

What you need:

* squares, circles, rectangles of black paper
* small objects such as pegs, small animals, beads, counters, cutlery, shape templates, small tools, brushes
* stones or bricks to hold the paper down
* a bright, sunny day

What you do:

1. Find a still, sunny spot on the ground.
2. Put down the paper and weight it down at the corners.
3. Choose some objects to place on the paper.
4. Leave the picture for an hour. When you return, take one of the objects off the paper and see if the sun has faded the paper round the object, leaving a dark outline shape.
5. You may need to adjust times for the brightness of the day.
6. Take the pattern inside and display it in the shade.

Some other ideas for experiments with sunshine:

- Put unbreakable mirrors on walls and even on the ground, so children can see reflections.
- Pour a pool of water on the ground and watch it evaporate. Draw a chalk circle round the pool every half hour.
- Use droppers and sprays to wet different surfaces and watch how the water evaporates.
- Wash the wheeled toys, or dressing up and dolls' clothes. Hang on a line to dry in the sun.
- Use chalk to draw round shadows and watch how they move during the day. Record the movement with playground chalk.

and some other things:

- Get some old glasses frames (always remove the lenses before using). Make these into coloured glasses by covering them with different colours of cellophane.
- Hang reflective things from trees, bushes, gutters and windows. Try CDs, streamers of foil or foil paper, prisms, foil trays, pie tins.
- Plant seeds that grow very quickly. Try mustard and cress, beans, peas, sunflowers.
- Freeze some unusual shapes and put them in an empty or full water tray for the children to explore. Try a wellington boot, a plastic glove, a jelly mould. Or freeze very small items in ice cubes. Try leaves or flowers.

Sunshine Art

Make flower windows

Thanks to Slough Centre Day Nursery, where I saw this idea.

What you need:

* small sticks and twigs; string, raffia or elastic bands
* white tissue paper
* very liquid white glue, brushes
* flowers, petals, leaves, grass

What you do:

1. Tie three or four sticks into a triangle or square.
2. Tear a piece of tissue big enough to cover your shape and overlap the edges. Paste it all over with glue.
3. Put the stick shape on top and fold the tissue over the frame.
4. Choose some flowers, leaves etc. to decorate your window.
5. Cover with another piece of tissue and paste all over this.
6. Hang up to dry with a string.

NB This activity looks (and is) messy, but the finished results are stunning! The white glue dries clear and the flowers and leaves glow through the tissue.

Some other ideas for sunshine art:

- Paint with liquid clay or mud on paths and walls. Wash away with plenty of water.
- Cut small shapes (fish, snakes, leaves, flowers) from cellophane, and leave them in the sun. Watch them twist and curl as they heat up.
- Try finger painting in the sun outside. See how the sun dries up the paint. Tape smooth paper to a table and pour the paint straight on.
- Pin a very big piece of paper to a fence or wall and work as a group to do a huge collaborative sunshine painting of everyone enjoying themselves, or make a drip, spray or splatter picture.

and some other things:

- Make some shadow puppets from black card and garden sticks. Hang a sheet on a fence and make shadow stories.
- Hang up some garden netting and make a nature screen by weaving leaves and flowers in the holes in the netting. Hang it up and look at the shadows the net makes.
- Make a sunny day house from garden canes tied at the top and covered with clear plastic. Or use the method opposite for making a flower bower tepee, tunnel or screen. You do exactly the same, but with bigger sheets of tissue. Don't forget to leave holes for windows and a door!

Make Weather Charts and Weather Stations

Make a weather chart

What you need:

* a painting easel or a big board
* a sheet of white card
* clear book covering film (sticky backed)
* thick felt pens

What you do:

1. Draw an outline of the days of the week (see below).
2. Cover the outline with sticky backed film.
3. Pin your weather chart to the easel or board.
4. Now you can either:
   a) get the children to fill in each square with a marker (dry wipe or permanent).
   b) do each day's weather picture on a Post-it or sticker.
   c) make some symbols (see end of book) and stick them on with blutack or self adhesive Velcro.
5. You could make a magnetic version on an old fridge door and attach symbols with magnetic tape. This version is also waterproof and can stay outside permanently.

Our Weather Chart

Monday	Tuesday	Wednesday
Thursday	Friday	Saturday
	Sunday	

Make a weather station

What you need:

* a strong post or a bird table
* empty plastic bottles
* ribbons, or fabric
* coat hangers
* cup hooks
* a thermometer
* wind chimes or bells
* feathers
* card, pens

What you do:

1. Set up your bird table or weather post.
2. Make sure the top is low enough for the children to reach and observe.
3. Make a rain gauge by following the instruction on page 35.
4. Make a wind sock by threading a tube of fabric on a ring of wire (made from a wire coat hanger).
5. Hang a thermometer from a hook.
6. Attach some wind chimes, feathers and streamers to catch the wind.
7. Make a sundial from card or rigid plastic sheet and stick it to the table.
8. Hang a clip board and pen from a hook, so children can record their observations.
9. Put a weather chart nearby, so children can record the daily weather.
10. Add small signs with weather symbols.

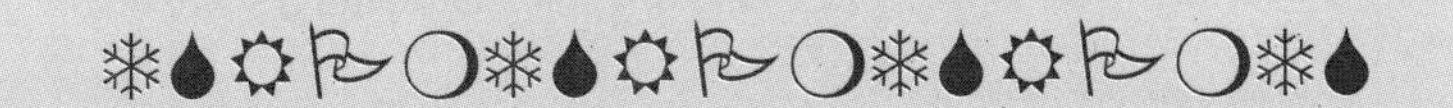

Games to play and songs to sing

Some weather games to play

Go puddle jumping.
Throw wet sponges at targets and into buckets.
Sweep rain in puddles and pools.
Make some paper planes and have a flying race.
Tie ribbons to your wrists and dance in the wind.
See how long you can keep a feather in the air by flapping or blowing.
Race boats down guttering or across ponds.
Race raindrops down window panes.
Paint a picture with water and watch it evaporate.

Some weather songs to sing

Snow, Snow Faster

Snow, snow faster,
Ally, ally aster,
The old woman is plucking her geese,
Selling feathers a penny a piece.

I Hear Thunder

I hear thunder,
I hear thunder,
Hark don't you?
Hark don't you?
Pitter, patter raindrops,
Pitter, patter raindrops,
I'm wet through,
So are you!

Rain on the Grass

Rain on the green grass,
And rain on the tree,
Rain on the house top,
But don't rain on me!

Red Sky at Night

Red sky at night,
Shepherd's delight,
Red sky in the morning,
Shepherd's warning.

Misty Moisty Morning

It was a misty, moisty morning,
And cloudy was the weather,
I saw an old man,
Dressed all in leather,
'How do you do,
And how do you do,
And how do you do again.'

Clouds

When clouds appear
Like rocks and towers
The earth is refreshed
By frequent showers.

I Can Sing a Rainbow

Red and yellow and pink and green,
Purple and orange and blue,
I can sing a rainbow,
Sing a rainbow,
Sing a rainbow too.

The North Wind Doth Blow

The north wind doth blow,
And we shall have snow,
And what will the robin do then,
Poor thing?
He'll sit in the barn,
And keep himself warm,
And tuck his head under his wing,
Poor thing.

The Sun has Got His Hat on

The sun has got his hat on,
Hip, hip, hip, hooray,
The sun has got his hat on,
And he's coming out to play.
So let us all be happy,
Shout 'Hip, hip, hip, hooray,'
The sun has got his hat on,
And he's coming out to play.

Rain, Rain, Go Away

Rain, rain, go away,
Come again another day,
All the children want to play.
OR:
Rain, rain, go to Spain,
Never show your face again.

It's Raining, It's Pouring

Its raining, its pouring,
The old man is snoring,
He went to bed,
And bumped his head,
And couldn't get up in the morning.

Role play in all weathers

Some ideas for role play

* Play firemen with hoses and buckets. Make a fire station in the shed and use the wheeled toys for rescue vehicles.
* Be a window cleaner, with a bucket and sponges, squeejees and cloths. Don't forget a step ladder and a bag for the money.
* Set up a painting and decorating business with roll of wallpaper, brushes and 'paint' (water). Paint the whole of the building and all the toys. Use sprays and rollers as well as buckets and brushes. Get some colour charts and sample books. You could even wallpaper the inside of the shed!
* Have a car wash with sponges, buckets, squeejees and leathers. Polish the bikes when you are done. Have a clip board for the car wash man and tickets for the cars waiting for a turn.
* Have a barbecue or a picnic with a parasol and waiters.

The Little Books Club

Little Books meet the need for exciting and practical activities which are fun to do, address the Early Learning Goals and can be followed in most settings. As one user put it

> *"When everything else falls apart I know I can reach for a Little Book and things will be fine!"*

Little Books Club members receive each <u>new</u> Little Book on approval at a reduced price as soon as it is published.

Examine the book at your leisure. Keep it or return it. You decide.

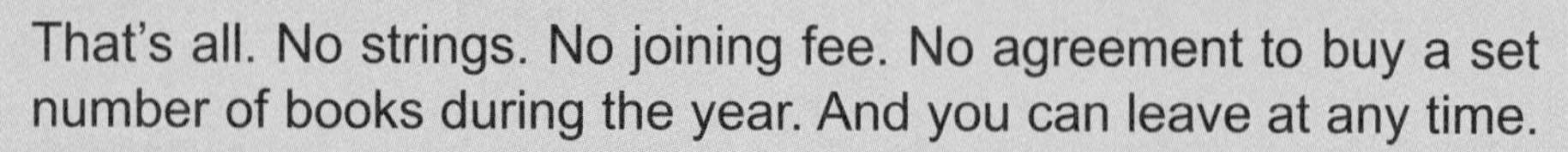

That's all. No strings. No joining fee. No agreement to buy a set number of books during the year. And you can leave at any time.

Little Books Club members receive -

- ♥ *each new Little Book on approval as soon as it's published*
- ♥ *a specially reduced price on that book and on any other Little Books they buy*
- ♥ *a regular, free newsletter dealing with club news and aspects of Early Years curriculum and practice*
- ♥ *free postage on anything ordered from our catalogue*
- ♥ *a discount voucher on joining which can be used to buy from our catalogue*
- ♥ *at least one other special offer every month*

There's always something in Little Books to help and inspire you!

Phone 0185 888 1212 for details